All Scripture references taken from the KJV unless otherwise indicated.

Dream Defilement, by Dr. Marlene Miles

Freshwater Press, 2023

ISBN: 978-1-960150-56-1

Paperback Version

Copyright 2023 by Dr. Marlene Miles

All rights reserved. No part of this book may be reproduced, distributed or transmitted by any means or in any means including photocopying, recording or other electronic or mechanical methods without prior written permission of the publisher except in the case of brief publications or critical reviews.

Table of Contents

While We Sleep 4
Why Don't I Remember My Dreams? 11
Defilement 14
Make It STOP! 22
Then The Night Comes 26
Levels of Defilement 33
Strange People & Strange Food 37
More Defilement 43
Bless That Food 48
You Cooked This for *Me?* 59
Be Sure To Remember 64
What Comes Out Defiles a Man 65
Defilement 3.0 69
Warfare Prayers 73
Prophecy 92
Spiritual Surgery 93
Christian books by this author 97

Dream
Defilement

Freshwater Press, USA

While We Sleep

Bless the Lord, oh my soul and all that is within me. Bless His holy name, (Psalm 103:1).

No weapon formed against me shall prosper.

(Isaiah 54:17)

Saints of God, at night we are to be meeting with God in our sleep while we are resting our bones, resting our souls, our minds, and our bodies. We are to meet up with the Most High God, Spirit to spirit. This is where God ministers to us. He talks with us; He leads us and guides us and delivers us. He informs us, teaches us, makes us new, renews us, renews covenant with us, and restores us and heals.

In the night hours.

Sometimes when those deep spiritual things are happening, they happen in dreams, or we learn about them in dreams because dreams are a mirror or picture of what is happening in the Spirit.

There are times when we get *other* dreams that are not from God. Sometimes we get dream pollution, or dream defilement.

Where does this dream defilement come from? Where do dreams come from? Dreams come from God. Dreams can come through your daily life; we may have silly dreams of men that don't mean anything at all.

Dreams can, also unfortunately, come from the devil.

> Dreams come through a multitude of business, and a fools voice is known by multitude of words, (Ecclesiastes 5:3).

God sometimes shows us things regarding our life in dreams such as things that we need to pray into manifestation, in the natural, and this way we **agree** with God. Or sometimes, in a dream, the Lord shows us things that the devil is planning, especially if you ask Him. *Show me the enemy's plan against my life.* God will show you so you can know how to pray, how to cancel the wicked plans of the devil.

Sometimes through a dream, the devil sets out things that he wants us to agree with. He tries to impersonate God, and he wants us to agree with things that we should not agree with. We should be sure not to agree with him. So we disagree with the devil, and we cancel the plans of the devil because he only wants to send our lives in the wrong direction. He only wants to steal, kill, and destroy.

In all of this, I hope you can hear that a dream really requires action. Every dream you dream requires action. Dreams are not just entertainment or frustration, or -- *whatever*. That's not what they are. It is a very dangerous thing for a believer not to do anything about a dream, and it's dangerous for a believer not to remember a dream,

John 14:26 says that the Holy Spirit is here to help our memory, and to bring all things back to our remembrance. So, if you can't remember something--, anything, you just ask the Holy Spirit. He will bring it back to your memory. Anything. Ask about dreams, ask to recall information that you studied for the last exam that you're taking--, that's not cheating. The Holy Spirit will bring a Word, a Rhema Word, back to your remembrance--, a prayer that you need to pray. Something you're supposed to know at work. The Holy Spirit is your Helper.

The Holy Spirit will give you driving directions when you can't get to your phone or if your GPS display is not working. Where's your phone anyway? The Holy Spirit knows where it is, just ask Him. He will tell you. Ask Him anything. He will bring *all things* back to your remembrance.

In Chapter 2 of the Book of Daniel, King Nebuchadnezzar had a dream, but he didn't remember the dream, and he also wanted the interpretation of the dream. So, he asked his psychic wise men about the dream. Of course, they couldn't interpret or recall the dream for him, but Daniel could, because it's a gift from God to be able to do such a thing.

The Holy Spirit will bring things to your remembrance. In Daniel's particular case the Lord brought Nebuchadnezzar's dream to Daniel and told him the interpretation of it.

If an evil king, a king of Babylon, had the wisdom to know that a dream is important, and that he needs to know what that dream means, how much more should we, saints of God, realize that God speaks to men in dreams.

Nebuchadnezzar's wise men aren't serving God. They can't do what Daniel can do by the Holy Spirit. We too, have the Spirit of God in us. We can know who to ask, who to seek, how to get Christian and Biblical interpretation of our dreams. So we know what actions to take, what prayers to make, what to cancel and how to cancel it. By this we can also know what things to pray into manifestation.

If an evil king knew, we should know much more.

In Genesis, Joseph interpreted the dream for evil Pharaoh who also had so-called wise men. They were just psychics with *familiar spirits*. They really couldn't interpret dreams, but they can be very convincing in whatever they tell you. They will have you believing that they know what they're talking about, either because they are conmen, or they are also deceived. There may be some truth in their words, but there may not be any truth to their interpretation. The *familiar spirit's* purpose in this is to tell you something that will steer your life in the wrong direction. So, do not listen to that.

You need Biblical Christian interpretation of your dreams.

Why Don't I Remember My Dreams?

What may cause you or me or a person not to remember their dreams?

Sin.

Prayerlessness; not praying. Ask God to help you remember your dreams as you go to sleep at night. Just ask Him.

Another blockage to remembering dreams is if we have been real trifling about getting into the Bible, reading the Word of God,

Also, any other type of spiritual pollution in our lives may block our recall of dreams.

It could be a witchcraft attack, sent by the devil, of course, as to why you can't remember your dreams.

Could be a lack of sleep that is causing blocked memories of dreams.

Too much stress in your life may block your dream recall.

Or not spending enough time with God may be the problem. You have to spend time with God because God is the person we're in relationship with. How can you be in a relationship with somebody without spending any time with them? OK, how will you be in a <u>good</u> relationship with somebody and you're only spending a little bit of time with them?

Let us now cleanse ourselves from all filthiness of the flesh and spirit, perfecting holiness in the fear of God. (2 Corinthians 7:1)

Defilement

A man's spirit can be defiled, his body can be defiled, his soul can be defiled, and his flesh can be defiled.

In our example from Daniel, Chapter 2, Nebuchadnezzar didn't seem worried about that—because he wasn't saved. He was more worried about his Kingdom, his power, and his own flesh.

As children of God, we should be concerned about defilement, about if our spirit is defiled, if our soul is defiled, if our body is defiled. We should be guarded not to defile *ourselves*, because that is a trick of the enemy. If we look at the Book of

Leviticus, starting around Chapter 18, there are a whole bunch of foul stuff in there that nobody should ever do. But the heart of man is wicked, and it really can't be trusted. So, the heart of man may devise wicked things.

Let's say for the purposes of this book that an evil arrow of lust has been sent to you and it hits the target. It hits a man. That evil arrow may have a man doing all kinds of things, thinking all kinds of lustful things. And the man may think that it's *him* not realizing that the devil is putting ideas and suggestions into his head. The devil is giving him inclinations and urges to do things that he thinks *he* wants to do. This man then begins to act out because of this evil arrow of *lust*.

This man might then go talk to his ignorant and possibly already demonized peers, his friends, his bro's. They will celebrate his great conquests and escapades, not realizing that it is a demon driving all this sin. They don't consider it sin because they think this is **manhood**. It's a demon. It is the demon of *lust*.

By accepting it and agreeing with it, they're inviting *more demons* into their life, into their body, into their mind, into their spirit, thereby defiling all three all the more. What these unsaved or this ignorant person may believe to be **normal** <u>becomes</u> their normal.

Now when he justifies himself and nobody tells him differently, he justifies himself by saying, oh, this is normal. He doesn't even know that it was wrong, and it was sin. He/they don't know that there is deliverance for this. There is freedom from this bondage that consumes a man's days, it consumes his nights, it consumes his life, even his thought life. It interferes with success. Sometimes he can't go to work because he's too tired from what he was doing last night.

He has self-justified it as normal. If you were born with a splinter in your finger, you will swear --you shouldn't swear, but you would swear that that splinter is supposed to be there, because it's always been there.

But in the case of this *spirit of lust*, it'll have a man who's defiled, begin doing the opposite of what God says to do. It may have him wanting to have relations with people he shouldn't be with--, his mother, stepmother, sisters, stepsisters, aunts on either side of his family, relatives by kin or marriage, daughters, daughter-in-law, sister-in-law, woman and her daughter, woman and her granddaughter. The neighbor's wife. It goes on.

Lust has no discernment and no class. It will try to have sex with anything and anyone. Leviticus tells of even worse…

All this talk has been about a man's waking hours, even though this book is about ***dream*** defilement--, and we will get there.

Sexual sins are grievous because you are sinning against your own body. Paul said he didn't know he was a sinner, until the Law was preached to him. Leviticus is one of the Books of the Law; the law is now being revealed to you, so you know what the sins are. Don't sin.

If you were hit with an evil, lustful arrow, it's overwhelming, really. You may feel it's impossible not to be lustful. You might want everything you see, from food, to relations, to gadgets, toys, even cars. It's because the demon of *lust* has convinced you that what **it** wants, **you** really want it. You may think you're having fun with that demon right now, but really, it isn't you. It really isn't you.

You were never like this before, and maybe you don't remember a time when you weren't like this, because maybe that memory has been erased from you. The devil is very tricky. He's very sneaky, and he has tactics.

So the devil may have a person thinking that this is the new, evolved you. This is the new cool, no longer stuck up you. You're no longer a prude, or a Bible thumper and the world is teaching you that you're *enlightened*. But this so-called enlightenment is not that at all, and it is not normal. It is not what God intended and it's not what you were made for. It is not normal.

It's not normal to desire things written in Leviticus 18, not to think on them, or do them. Doing them *is* the sin, it is the transgression, and it brings the iniquity to the 3rd and 4th generations of your bloodline, if you're saved. If your bloodline is not saved iniquity can visit for 10 to 14 generations!

I talked to a guy once who proclaimed his lusty ways. He said he was just putting it out there. He celebrated his lustful thinking and conquests. ...I know *to me?* He said he really wanted more experiences in life, he wanted something more, something more exciting, he said. Exciting? I say, Sinful.

No, thank you. I don't want any of that because it's not normal. It's not normal for a man to behave that way and to have those kinds of lusts, or even worse. For this guy not to be aware that it's not normal and that it is *lust* and is not of God--, not even of man but of the devil tells how far gone this man is.

Hey but, *Players gonna play and demons gonna manifest.* We need to know when a demon is talking, and not try to make it something acceptable in our head. It's a demon; only a demon would say stuff *like that.* At that time, I probably should have asked that demon its name, but it wasn't a deliverance call.

Make It STOP!

SIN HAS A COST. Sin has to and will be paid for. If the sinner doesn't pay for sin today, there's tomorrow, or at some other time where payment will be exacted. If you don't pay for it, then your children, your grandchildren, your great grandchildren will pay—for **YOUR** sin. By the time you have grands--, and great grands, you may have forgotten the sins of your youth. You may be preaching holiness, even, Bible thumping, by then, but your generations won't escape just because *you* forgot about it and started preaching holiness--, **without repentance**. Hear the Word of the Lord today.

Sometimes the devil saves up that sin card that you just dealt him by agreeing with his sinful ideas and suggestions. And he may take that card, add it to some other cards and then just wait for the day, the time, the hour when he can deal the most harm back to you and to your bloodline.

So once you sinned, but nothing seemed to happen to you, you may think, *Oh, I got away with it.* You think nothing happened because no one in the natural world saw you. Baby, EVERYBODY in the spirit world saw you. EVERYBODY. The devil is not Omnipresent like God, but he has henchmen and *monitoring spirits* watching for sinners that he can trap and devour. Don't be one of them.

The heart of man is wicked; he devises a lot of wicked things, and the devil gives suggestions that men don't even realize are not even their own thoughts. Then he watches you fall into his traps.

You are at least *trying* to obey the laws of God, *right*? If not, I must ask, who's running your life? Because a demon will run your feet straight to mischief and then straight to Hell. In Hell, it's over; there are no do-overs.

So, the enemy of God wants to defile a man--, all mankind actually. He wants to violate, pollute, and contaminate him, disgrace, stain, tarnish him. In so doing, the devil doesn't mind destroying a man, making him impure, and filthy. That's what defilement is. The devil's purpose in defiling a man is to steal, kill, and destroy.

Steal what? Destroy what? God-given gifts, virtues, a man's destiny, his future, his successes and to make that man's life suck. The devil wants to make a man's life difficult or impossible. He wants to make it a life of sorrow and affliction. He won't mind giving you memory loss, to make you forget that you are a man and, that you are a child of God. He wants you to forget. He wants you to think you're a lustful party animal or a pitiful weakling.

The devil hates you. By defiling a man, he also wants to make you unproductive, damaging or damning the natural as well as the spiritual fruit of your body. The devil will try to block, damage, or destroy your ministry and your purpose of being here on Earth; he hates you.

So that's what I call daytime defilement. You're awake while all this is happening to you. Hopefully all of us are aware enough, that is spiritually *woke* enough to make right decisions about what we'll do and what we will not do as it pertains to sin.

But, even while saved, every day, we must **choose** if we're going to serve God or if we are going to serve *not*-God.

Then The Night Comes

Then the night comes. The same attacks keep happening, only this time in your sleep. At night you still have to fight suggestions, coercions, leads, promptings, and tricks of the devil. Yes, even while you're asleep, you're still being tested. Asleep is the time that your spirit man is supposed to be communing with **God**--, Spirit to spirit. Times of refreshing in the Lord, times of revitalization, healing, renewal, restoration. Spirit-to-spirit hooking up with God is what is supposed to be happening.

When we go to sleep, our spirit should be making a beeline to the Throne of God to **worship God**. But where *do* we go at night? Where do you go? Where does your spirit go at night? Your spirit doesn't sleep, so WYD, WYA? *What (are) you doing? Where you at?*

Likewise, all these filthy dreamers defile the flesh, (Jude 1:8a).

The Devil sends dream criminals into our lives. They're assigned to bring *dream pollution*. They are evil *spirits*. They know you. They know me. They have studied us since we were born. They know what we like and what we don't like. They know what we are likely to do, and what we are not likely to do. Their goal is to trap and ensnare us, and to compromise our lives.

They show up, right when we are about to have some great natural successes in our life or spiritual promotion from God.

They show up to defile us, because if they can defile us, that causes God to turn His back on us, even if just for that day. Thank God for repentance and do-overs, on this side of Heaven, but the Word says, men ought to always repent.

At night, man is minding his own business, trying to get some sleep. Here come some dream criminals to defile him.

Even in the natural in our awake life, there's sabotage. If you say you want to fast, here comes somebody catering a whole lunch, and it's free and it's delicious. The food and the fasting are quickly gone.

Or you decide you're going to make better choices for your life; you're not going to do this that or the third anymore. Here comes somebody with a free gift. Inviting you to go do this, that or the third. It's a temptation to do exactly what you are trying not to do.

It's to defile you.

Dream criminals show up to defile you and God hates defilement of any kind.

To the defiled, all things are defiled. And to the pure, all things are pure, (Titus 1:15).

God deals with us according to the condition of our heart, but Jesus said that it's not what goes into a man, it's what comes out of him that defiles him. Well, anything that gets into you, when it comes out, it will be wrapped with your *brand*. If your heart is evil, if there's any root of bitterness in it, if it is unforgiving, if it's defiled, sullied, dirty, soiled, then what comes out of you will have your *brand* on it. For example, if someone tells you something and you repeat it, it will have your *flavor* on it when you retell it. That's why gossip is so dangerous as it goes from person to person, flavor to flavor, from distortion to distortion.

But you're asking--, and I'm asking the Lord, how can a dream defile us? How can that be our fault? I mean, it's a dream, for goodness' sake.

Yeah, but it's our spirit, man and we're responsible for what our spirit man does--, even at night.

In a dream, it could be that you have wondered, did you do that or not? Depends on your memory of that dream. If the devil has covered your memory, you may not have a clue as to what happened to you or your spirit man that night--, any night.

If you have prayed to the Lord to make sure you always remember every dream, you will know and be in position to do something about dreams that need daytime attention. **Every dream needs daytime attention.**

If it happens and you don't remember that happened, then the door is open for whatever happened to keep happening, possibly to your detriment.

The devil uses every opportunity to erase your memory of your dreams. After that he can do whatever he wants. And you still may never know what's going on. In the night, you may be ***accepting defilement*** and not even realizing it. This is how a person can be defiled and that is how you are responsible for what happened in the dream if you accepted or agreed with it. Not doing anything about choices presented to you means you accept it.

As a rule, I cancel every evil dream every morning as soon as I wake up – whether I remember a dream or not. I cancel every demonic dream even before I know what it means. Now that it's canceled, I can take my time talking to the Holy Spirit about it to find out what each thing means in it, so I can ultimately know how to pray for the best Godly outcomes and advantage to my life.

https://www.youtube.com/watch?v=ktrpFtLOTgM&t=117s

Looking at the words, *defiled* and *deviled*, there's only one letter off. Let that be a clue to all of us.

Levels of Defilement

If your spirit is defiled, so is your soul. If your soul (mind) is defiled, and not dealt with, then there goes your body. It's defiled too. Defilement leads to condemnation, and condemnation leads to destruction. Please, if any of this is happening to you, that should let you know that the devil really is out to get you. We all have to work out our Salvation with fear and trembling. We can't just sit on our haunches all day and do nothing, saying, *"The Lord knows my heart."*

Yeah, God knows your heart. And you have to know your own heart, too.

What evil is in it? The heart of man is wicked. God says He will not always strive with us. Know your own heart. How will you know your own heart, if you don't know what you are doing in your dreams? If you don't know what your spirit man is doing in the night hours, you will not know *all* of who you are.

Your spirit man is the very essence of you. The body will die and decay. The soul became alive with the breath of God. Your spirit has been living forever and will continue to live forever even after the breath of God has expired for this life. **You must <u>know</u> your spirit man and build your spirit up on this side of Heaven.**

A heart can be defiled, and the person may still be going about life --so happy, not even aware that he is defiled. The clues to defilement may only be in your dreams that you either ignore or don't remember. Else, you could live in error and not even be aware of defilement, until it hits you in the natural, where it really hurts.

Even in the dream we can be defiled by trickery, ignorance, rebellion. We could agree with the devil, agreeing with his violence, and we could defile ourselves that way, in the dream.

In the daytime too, there are people with the *defiling spirits* on them that can be transferred to others. There is such a thing as spiritual transference, most often by intimate relations such as adultery and fornication. But sometimes it's just by association. We're supposed to shun such people.

Women, you meet a guy and he's a bad boy; he's exciting. He's daring; he'll do almost anything. We can't use this as an excuse to go buck wild with that wild guy and then think we can just blame it on the man. No, **you** are responsible for your own actions. If he is a defiled man, **<u>you</u>** will become defiled when you *get with him*. Demons transfer, and most often the woman takes on the man's nature, whether she's legally married to him or not, whether the relationship is short or long-term.

Strange People & Strange Food

Spirit food is strange food. Eating strange food in the dream is defilement. Spirit food and/or beverage is defilement; spirits don't eat.

Eve defiled herself by eating something she wasn't supposed to eat. Even if Adam didn't eat in the Garden, he would have had occasion to *get with* Eve. She was his wife; he would have gotten defiled anyway if she is defiled, and vice versa. If Adam had committed the first sin the same would have applied to Eve. It works both ways.

When one in a couple defiles him- or herself, say *in the streets*. They can bring home all kinds of evil, both naturally and spiritually speaking, and transfer it to their spouse.

The Word says that the man who gets with a harlot becomes one with that harlot. (1 Corinthians 6:16).

A defiled person is dirty, soiled, stained, in the eyes of God. They become almost like a second-hand Christian. The purpose of defilement is to push God away from you, to push Heaven away from you, to close your Heaven, to make you stink in the eyes of God.

You may not be actively sinning in your dream life, but you could be passively getting defiled, doing things in the dream that you would NEVER do in your awake life. If you are not doing anything about dream defilement, then it is as though you accept it, and so it stands. That is not free sex in the dream; that is defilement.

Dreams are pictures of things that are happening in the spirit realm. You need to know what is happening. Is your spirit man getting *busy* with all kinds of entities and masquerades? If that's happening, how are you maintaining yourself with sanctification and honor?

Marriage in the dream is defilement. You wouldn't need to re-marry your own spouse in a dream. That is a masquerade. That is a stranger (demon) in a mask that you will accept. It could be *spirit spouse*. **https://a.co/d/68RUUDo**

Sex in the dream is defilement. You think this dream is of God who is showing you your new spouse that you've been praying for. Trust me, whatever you're having sex with, in the dream, is a masquerade; it is a demon. This demon has applied some face that you will accept, usually something pretty good looking.

God would not have you having sex in the dream; it is defilement. We will not marry or have spouses in Heaven, because we will be all spirit. God will not have you having sex in the dream. God doesn't, God would not have you having sex with any "person" that you're not married to. If God is showing you a spouse, or future spouse, He will address union, covenant, and purpose with the two of you, giving you the vision for your marriage, not indulging you in the flesh part of the relationship. That's not God.

Come on, we've all been to prophetic services. How many prophets have you ever heard give a *thus saith the Lord* prophecy, and it's about sex, or flesh? It's about how good looking or rich your husband will be. That's not God.

Any sex in any gender combination in the dream is defilement. In the dream sex act, the demon assumes the face, and the body that you *may* accept to defile you. It's never what it seems; if it's the devil, it's always a trap.

Sometimes the demon may not even assume an acceptable face or image, but it will force the defilement. If this defilement has gone on so long that the door is wide open, all protections may be gone, unless you're prayerful and asking God to help you.

We need deliverance; it is the children's bread. Do not be embarrassed or ashamed. Seek deliverance if that is happening or has happened to you.

Certain dreams are defilement. Sometimes dreams spill over into the natural. Men, God hates spilled seed. So, what does the devil do? The devil tries to promote exactly what God hates. *Spirit spouse* is often responsible for dream or morning spilled seed; that is not free sex. Defilement has a cost. Often, it's a future cost, but it has a cost.

So a person is defiled. What happens in the natural? Their prayers aren't answered. Their heaven can be shut. Their glory is delayed. The promises of God aren't available to the defiled, and now you're a candidate for more defilement, even as a Christian. People think just because you are saved nothing can happen to you. Even as a Christian, you are most interesting to the devil because you *are* a Christian.

More Defilement

Emissions on the body, emissions on the bed from so-called dreams is defilement. The fallen angels looked upon the daughters of men and saw that they were fair, and they married them, (Genesis 6:6). God does not wink at human emissions that fall to the ground as in the case of Onan (Genesis 38) not providing seed to Tamar, as God had instructed him. Under the Law in the OT, Onan was killed.

We are under Grace--, perhaps we don't die naturally--, immediately, but we risk demonic captivity every time we violate spiritual laws and covenant.

There are other signs of defilement in the dream. If you see yourself in the dream sleeping around animals that the Bible declares unclean that is defilement.

Sleeping around dirty animals is defilement, dirty birds, owls, vultures, scorpions, snakes--, unclean animals and insects. Spit and saliva in the dream is defilement. Dreaming of swimming in dirty water or drinking dirty water is defilement.

No dream at all, or a covered dream is defilement. Not remembering your dream at all is defilement.

Some people say that God seals some dreams for future dates to reveal it to you. I don't agree with that. You have to pray, seriously, pray and ask God about that. Because the devil is likely hiding your dream from you. You may have agreed to something in the dream that you need to cancel or deal with.

This tactic has happened to me. I may have a dream from God and it's a really good dream, but right before I wake up a dream criminal, or a dream manipulator will throw another ridiculous or alarming dream at me to try to make me alarmed and forget the dream that God sent. Its evil goal was to make me forget the God-inspired dream.

The devil is a devil; he is very sneaky.

- Father, I pray that when I have a dream that I need to remember, wake me up so I can remember it, write it down, and take action to deal with it accordingly, in the Name of Jesus.

Oh yeah, there's more dream defilement such as being attacked physically, sexually, being touched, caressed, or kissed in the dream by unknown people. If you find yourself naked in a dream, fully or partially, that's defilement. If you see other people naked in the dream, that's defilement.

This prayer has been very effective for me:

https://www.youtube.com/watch?v=0Q_lqy6h53Q&t=16554s

Incisions and injections are all horrible defilements in the dream.

Seeing yourself in a coffin in the dream is defilement. Seeing dead bodies in the dream is defilement.

Nightmares are defilement. Dirty clothes and filthy garments are defilements.

Bed wetting is defilement. Seeing sores or boils are defilement. God hates all defilement. The purpose of defilement is to keep God out of your life, to possibly close your heaven, and keep the glory of God out of your life, and to make your life difficult.

God turns His back on the defiled and any defilement, God turns His back on sin. If it were not for God's forgiving nature and every morning His tender mercies, we would all be in a world of hurt. (Read and pray Psalm 124).

Filthy dreams are defilement. You may be thinking, when I went to sleep last night, I wasn't planning to have filthy dreams. I wasn't thinking anything filthy. I'm not even a filthy thinker. You know you are not a perv. But some demonic dream attacks you in your sleep, and it is filthy. You wake up feeling shocked, stunned, and horrible. You may claim that you are innocent because you didn't *plan* or encourage an attack, but you were. You've been defiled, even violated, so you need to check yourself. Remember, no curse can alight without a cause. Check your spiritual life, your prayer life. Are you reading and studying the Bible?

Check your family background; were you born into an evil foundation, and received an evil inheritance? If so this could be why these doors are open against you for defilement, and/or dream, defilement.

Bless That Food

There are so many more defilement dreams. You could study this every day and still keep learning things because the devil is busy. He is always inventing new ways to do bad things to mankind.

A sure defilement is eating in the dream. And I remind us of our foundational Scriptures.

Bless the Lord oh my soul and all that is within me, (Psalm 103:1)

No weapon formed against me shall prosper.

Isaiah 54:17

As I was praying, preparing for this and meditating on the Word of God, conviction from the Lord came to me, about eating in the dream, WHILE I was eating in the natural, as I popped a snack into my mouth.

I was having something that most people would consider a snack. I hate that word, *snack*, because it's like saying when you get some food for the road, that it's got special characteristics. No, it's still food, filled with calories, preservatives, and who knows what else. But we use the word, *snack* to kind of justify road food or anything we probably shouldn't eat, or that we may sneak to eat.

We may be thinking, *It's not so much; it's a small portion.* It's just gonna be a little bit, but it won't hurt us. We're all guilty. So we call this thing a *snack*, but again, this snack is just one letter and one position away from *snake*. This may not be good for us.

Anyway, as I was popping what I considered a delicious morsel into my mouth, I realized that I had not prayed over it. I hadn't blessed this snack. Because I'm thinking it's just a snack, something I'll have quickly, like a candy, a gum, a mint, or a cookie.

I remember one time being at an event and appalled that I was at dinner with people who had beverages, soft drinks, and appetizers but they didn't **pray** over the food until the main course got there. At that time I was thinking, *What kind of infidels are these?*

Back then I was judging them, but look at me now. What about me? I hadn't blessed the ***snack***. And that's when the Lord revealed to me that the night caterers, the evil satanic night feeders, the dream criminals that bring us food to eat in our dreams, those who are responsible for defiling mankind with eating in the dream, can be so effective against us because certain doors are open. We may be prayerless. We may be careless. And that lack of discipline tells on us in our dream life.

Night caterers can be successful *because* we're not blessing our food.

If you blessed everything that you ate and drank in the daytime, you would be so <u>**programmed**</u> to **bless** anything that *looked* like it was going to be food. If anything was coming anywhere near your mouth, you would automatically, even in your dream, your spirit man would start blessing that night food – that evil food.

As a matter of course, we don't bless the food that we eat when we are awake. **That food also defiles us.**

When we do not bless the food that we eat in the daytime, that food also defiles us. You know you have an aversion to ungrateful people. So, why wouldn't God notice that we are not grateful for food and other blessings? We need to bless our food, water, beverage, anything that goes into the temple of the Holy Spirit. Our body is the temple of the Lord. We need to bless everything that goes near, comes near it, goes in it-- all food, everything that goes in the body, whether it's evil food or if it's if we take in food inadvertently that we don't even know that it's evil.

You may be eating food that is dedicated to idols and not even know it--, in the wake state *and* in the dream. We don't know where that food has been, or who made it. And we don't know with what *intent* they made it and with what intent they're giving it to you.

You are the temple of the Holy Spirit. If you think of an actual temple with an outer court, an inner court, and the Holy of Holies, realize how close food, as it goes through your esophagus and into your stomach, how close that is to your heart. Your heart is the seat of your being, the center of the core of your being.

As the center of your being, let's say your heart is your Holy of Holies. You're not gonna let just anything in there or near your most sacred place, *are you?*

The Scripture says that we enter into His gates with Thanksgiving and into His courts with praise. Saint of God, your mouth is the gate. My mouth is a gate, and we are defiling our own body if we let just anything into our gate *without* Thanksgiving, without discernment, without knowing exactly what that something is.

Ask God in prayer, *what's this? Should I let this go through my gates?*

We need to bless our food, beverages, candy, gum, snacks, mints, cookies, potato chips--, everything. And if we were to bless everything we eat and drink, we would get in the habit, a real habit of blessing everything we eat and drink, **even in the dream.**

Thank You, Lord, even in the night we will be trained to bless any beverage, food, snack, any and everything that was placed in our hands or near us or in the dream that even *resembled* food.

So that means that if some evil entity, some *guardian demon*, some night raider, some evil dream criminal or whatever is assigned to defile us by feeding us in the dream, every time food or beverage came near us, you begin to bless it, calling on the Name of Jesus, how long do you think that night criminal, will be around?

The King of Glory steps in because you just prayed. You now pray over everything. Yep, everything. Because you don't know where anything came from or who touched it. You don't know who's prayed over it already. You don't know who's issued incantations over it already, especially food, spiritually speaking.

Naturally speaking, what if you're eating food from a dirty cook? What if the cook has unwashed hands, or licks his fingers, or doesn't use tasting spoons or, sings or talks over the food the entire time they are cooking or plating it? How much of their spittle will be in your food? PRAY, against the spray.

The average restaurant, do you think their decorations are cute? It's all up there for you to see. It's not cute. They're telling you who they are by their décor which is really an altar of the things they believe in and worship, especially at the cash register. They're telling you who they worship. They worship these idol *gods* for success and for money. When you pay, you are putting **your** money on their altars and you're patronizing their little g *gods*. You are giving sacrifices to the altars of false and evil *gods*.

Food that's been sacrificed to idols should never be consumed by man, especially a man of God.

And in the dream, <u>what</u> do you think the devil is dishing out? What do you think he's giving you anyway? *What is the food that you eat in the dream? You don't know what it is.* What is this *food* that you're eating? And why would the devil FEED you? He's not your host at a fancy dinner party.

I say all this because it's happened to me. Lord, help me, in the Name of Jesus. And that is the *why* of this book. I'm praying that it won't happen to you. If it does, I pray it will stop, in the Name of Jesus.

What is this *alleged* food, this dream food--, what is it? It has no taste. It has no texture. What is it? We don't know--, *or do we?*

Then in the natural, snack and food companies, want to make sales. They want to be successful. How do we know what *god* they are praying to? Some people want success in this life at any cost. They don't even believe that there's a price to pay in eternity. So they may do ***anything*** for success and money. **We may be eating *their* food.** Bless that food.

You better bless everything. Everything. We cannot assume that everyone is Christian and that what they're dishing up has been blessed by God, or even that God has been asked to be in any of the entire process of bringing an item to market. They just want to make sales.

You need to bless the medicines that go in your body before you take them--, over the counter meds and prescription meds. Bless everything that the Lord approves of you having; bless it anyway.

Either way, you stay prayerful or end up curbing your eating all day long. Either way, it's good for you.

You Cooked This for *Me?*

Foods that have been especially prepared for--, I don't know--, **you** --while you're awake can also be concerning. You've been invited for a meal, and it has been pre-programmed with enchantments, charms, spells, vexes, hexes, hoodoo, voodoo, and Lord knows what else. This food has been **cursed,** the person who's doing all this may think, they just love you, they're in love with you, and it's a **love potion**. They're enchanting and casting a love spell over you because they want you to fall in love with them too.

They are summoning demons. Don't eat this.

Love potions are witchcraft. Men, especially --, if it's red you had better pray over that spaghetti sauce. Men, you've been invited to someone's home for a home cooked meal. You're on a date? You might be so distracted that you think the food is a means to an end and the food doesn't even matter. Well, the food is a means to an end, and the food REALLY matters.

Your hostess insists that you sit in some certain chair. You have to sit just in **that** chair. You had better watch it. Only that certain chair and then on top of it you were served a red meal.

Some may be saying, it *don't* take all that. Maybe this message is not for you… *right now*. If you are fortunate enough to never be surprised at what people do to you, what people will do to have their own way, no matter what *you* want, then thank You Lord.

I want to say in a not so gentle way that since your birth you've probably been told, *Get that out of your mouth,* more than anything else in your entire life. Remember what your momma told you, because waking meals that are cursed as well as dream defilement by food is also spirit, soul, and body defilement.

The devil is handing us a weapon, that he has fashioned against our destiny, against our life and purpose; he has disguised it as food, and we are swallowing it, like cartoon characters.

Lord, God, help us. What is wrong with us? Help us Lord, so that nothing will be wrong with us. Help us so that we will not just accept or eat things that are handed to us.

Our spirit doesn't need food. It is ludicrous for us to eat in the dream.

People of God, **when a person is experiencing strange movements in their body – that is a result of spiritual food that has been eaten in the dream.** It is a sign that spiritual food has begun to work *against* a person, against their health. Eating in the dream is devastating.

So you, as a child of God need to purpose to BLESS EVERYTHING that touches you. Everything that comes near you. Anything that goes in your mouth--, bless it. Use the Name of Jesus, the Blood of Jesus. Cover it with the Blood of Jesus and once you've trained your spirit man to speak and invoke the Blood of Jesus whenever you even SEE food let it be a trigger. You see food, start praying so the night caterers will leave you alone.

Once spirit food is into your body the enemy will start to use it against you, your health, success, promotion, life, marriage, children--, every part of your life.

But you need to bless everything that touches you, everything that comes near you that is destined for your mouth. Bless it. And be sure to use the Name of Jesus, and the Blood of Jesus. Once you have trained your spirit man to speak and invoke the Blood of Jesus, whenever food or beverage arrives, the night caterers, dream criminals, evil caterers, or whatever you choose to call them, will flee from you.

In the Name of Jesus bind those demons and evil entities when in spiritual warfare mode.

Be Sure To Remember

Dreams that we don't remember are dreams of defilement. God does not wipe or cover our dreams. If your dream is lost, the devil did it. If the devil did it, he doesn't want you to know something that he did to you in the dream or something you agreed to in the dream.

Ask for Godly dream interpretation. Don't ask a psychic or a secular online interpreter. Lord! Don't ask a witch or a fortune teller. They get their information from *familiar spirits* from the second heaven. What you'll hear will be spiritual, but it's not of God.

What Comes Out Defiles a Man

Jesus said it's not what goes into a man that defiles him, but what comes out, (Mark 7:14-23). What goes in will come out eventually, and it will be changed by *you* while it's in there or going *through you*. We have no way to metabolize spiritual "food." So it stays in there until it is nullified, rendered harmless and/or spiritually removed. What it's doing while it's there are both important things to consider.

While spirit food and its pollution are in a human being, it could be affecting a person either, not at all, mildly, or in a devastating way. Spirit food is placed as a remote, internal **weapon** that the devil has formed to use at will to hurt a person. Or, worse.

This pollution could be affecting the actions you take, or your way of thinking. It could corrupt your mind, your heart, or your belief system in some way, and so it changes what comes out of you. It is what comes out of a man that defiles him.

Adam and Eve were defiled by the serpent, and they were deceived, and they were defiled. If either one had gotten defiled, they are married--, once they have relations, one is going to defile the other one.

If you hook up with somebody who is defiled, you will become defiled. I call a person's defilement, *spiritual dirt*. If somebody has spiritual dirt on them and you *get with them* in an intimate kind of a way, you will get it too. You will pick it up.

The devil defiles a person, but if they spread the filth, then the devil is even happier.

The devil defiles, if not all at once, he'll do it in stages and steps, by degrees. A little bit of this, little bit of that. Open the door for this, and then the next thing.

The only way we can get over this is to repent to the Lord, receive Salvation and ask that He put a new heart, a clean heart in us. In so doing, we can be saved. If we are already saved and defiled, we are again forgiven by God's tender mercies toward us. But we must ask; men ought to always pray.

The weapons we swallow are internal and have more potential for damage than the stuff that's on the outside of us. The number one source of defilement is food because most people eat multiple times a day. Also, when people are hungry they can be in the flesh, turning off discernment and moving in survival mode. They just want to EAT!

Food in the dream and in the natural-
-. unblessed food, and food that's dedicated to idols is the worst thing any of us can ever put in our mouths.

Defilement 3.0

Another source of defilement comes from the words that we speak. Our own words can be very defiling; we can defile *ourselves* even while trying to defile others--, cursing others.

Blood, all human waste, and reproductive emissions, improper and illegal sexual emissions are defiling. Masturbation is defiling.

Piercings, cuttings, incisions, acupuncture, and drugs are defiling.

Evil items in your house are defiling.

Unfortunately, some people have been born into a defiled foundation, an evil foundation. A lot of people are born into things that they don't even suspect until they begin to feel the pains of it. At that point they may start to search for answers. They do a deep dive, hopefully into the dumpster of their ancestors' lives to try to backtrack, sleuth, and figure out what in the world this ancestor, or these ancestors did that caused what's happening, and how to undo it or get rid of it.

How do we get out of spiritual dumpsters?

Once defiled, the glory of God departs, and we become like secondhand Christians. We must be diligent about the things that we do, accept and hold on to in our lives, because even a root of bitterness in us, because of some perceived or *real* hurt can still bring defilement.

- Lord, forgive us for unforgiveness and bitterness, in the Name of Jesus.

Once defiled that person is marked, spiritually speaking. If you have ever found bruises, scrapes, and scratches on your body in the natural, and you know that night you were by yourself and nothing like that should be on your body, you need to seek deliverance. Most often that is *spirit spouse*, the spirit of vexation, or some other tormenting demon that's actually putting hands on you. Once a demon starts visiting you like that they will continue until you **STOP** them. Seek deliverance.

Visitation from demons is defilement.

Constant defilement will drive the anointing of God away from your life and may close Heaven over you. It will delay your destiny or maybe reroute it all together. It could cause your destiny to be stolen. It can make your heart sick, lead to depression, sadness, lack, poverty and may destroy your life.

Seek deliverance.

Repent.

If you cannot find a deliverance minister--, they are not a dime a dozen--, start somewhere starting with the Word of God. Start in prayer, on your knees. Fast. You can find some good deliverance ministers even online. If you can't find one in the natural, pray for the mercy of God and He will deliver you. Resist the devil, and he will flee from you, the Word says.

Warfare Prayers

As I begin these prayers, I cover myself, my family and all my belongings with the precious Blood of Jesus Christ.

Father, in the Name of Jesus, every plant that you did not plant, let it be uprooted in the Name of Jesus.

Thank You, Lord that I'm born again. Put a new heart in me. Renew my heart, Renew my spirit so no curse will alight on me again, in the Name of Jesus.

Holy Spirit, fight for me. Holy Spirit Fire fight these defiling dreams and every perpetrator in the evil dream and every cause that brings an evil dream to me, in Jesus' Name.

Thank You Lord, my prayers are heard, I pray without ceasing in the Spirit and with understanding.

Lord, thank You that I am not defiled in the night hours, in the Name of Jesus.

I put on the whole armor of God. I don't know where my dreams may take me, where my spirit may go, what evil may be trying to summon me. Any evil altar that is calling my name, or calling my spirit, Blood of Jesus answer for me.

Lord, welcome me to the Throne of God to worship You in Spirit and in Truth. Bless the Lord, Oh my soul ,and all that is within me.

Any evil altar that is calling my name, or my spirit, Lord Jesus answer for me. Holy Ghost Fire answer for me; light that altar on fire and destroy it, in the Name of Jesus.

Lord be with me in the night hours, Lord, be with me in the dream, You give your Beloved sleep. Cause me to dwell in safety, and not be defiled, in the Name of Jesus.

Lord, speak to me in the dream. Let my dreams be Holy Ghost inspired and not devil-influenced, in the Name of Jesus.

Lord, let me connect with you Spirit-to-spirit, let me make my covenant with You, Lord God, in the Name of Jesus.

Lord, I ask You to help me to remember my dreams. Wake me up after any important dream, in the Name of Jesus.

Lord, I ask You for proper interpretation of every dream (and vision), if not send me to correct sources to find out what my dreams mean, in the Name of Jesus.

Thank You, Lord for delivering us from the defilement of eating in the dream, and/or sex in the dream, in Jesus' Name.

Bless the Lord, Oh my soul and I command that **all that is within me** to bless His holy name.

I come against the evil arrows of the wicked intended to defile me. Let them receive the Blood of Jesus and return to sender.

Father, as I practice the disciplines of the faith, study, prayer and fasting, I bring my flesh under subjection. Deliver me from all defilement, whether in the natural or in the dream, in the Name of Jesus.

Thank You Jesus, that You came to get us out of our polluted blood, out of our pollution, out of our sin, out of our defilements, in the Name of Jesus.

Lord, Father, I command every dream, every imagination, thought, vision, that is contrary to my life's scroll, my destiny and progress to be cancelled in the Mighty Name of Jesus Christ.

To every evil, stubborn power troubling my life and destiny in the dream, God arise and let all my enemies be scattered, in Jesus' Name.

Every devouring spirit and defrauding spirit snatching away what belongs to me through dreams, catch fire now and burn to ashes, in the Name of Jesus.

My Father, every demonic ladder the enemy is using in my dreams to interrupt my purpose, blessings and destiny, break now by fire in the Mighty Name of Jesus.

Every demon of immorality, every dream criminal assigned against me come out now, in the Name of Jesus.

Lord, come into my life and take control, in the Name of Jesus.

Holy Ghost Fire, come upon my life. My life receive fire, become Fire, in Jesus' Name.

Messengers of Satan in my life, die in the Name of Jesus.

Every yoke against my health, break, in the Name of Jesus.

Bless the LORD, oh my soul and I command that all that is within me, Bless His Holy Name.

Every projection, every astral projection, every spirit husband, spirit wife, spirit spouse, all witchcraft be arrested in the Name of Jesus.

Every enchantment, incantation, charm, hex, voodoo, hoodoo, spell, curse and sorcery, be nullified and canceled, in Jesus' Name.

All assignments against me in my dreams, back to sender, NOW, in the Name of Jesus.

Dark strangers release me by fire, in the Name of Jesus.

Any power attempting to defile the Temple of the Holy Spirit, attempting to defile my body, be scattered, in the Name of Jesus.

Every power of defilement afflicting my life, scatter, in the Name of Jesus.

Every power standing by to mock me, die, in the Name of Jesus.

Any power standing by to laugh at me, be scattered, in the Name of Jesus.

My spirit man reject defilement, in the Name of Jesus.

Bless the LORD, oh my Soul and ALL that is within me, I command you to bless the Lord, Bless His Holy Name.

Any angel of darkness chasing good things away from me, be arrested today. Be put in irons and cast into the Abyss, in Jesus' Name.

My Father, arise for my sake, and embarrass my enemies, in the Name of Jesus.

My body, my soul, my spirit, receive the Fire of the Holy Ghost, in the Name of Jesus.

Let my enemies be put to shame by the power in the Blood of Jesus.

My hands, hear the Word of the Lord, possess my possessions, in Jesus' Name.

Every agenda of darkness, I cancel you by Fire, in the Name of Jesus.

Lord God of Elijah, Arise and let my story change for good, in the Name of Jesus.

Lord, break me loose from every *spirit* that wants to defile me, in the Name of Jesus.

Lord, put the sword of the Spirit between me and any dream criminal, any night raider, any spirit spouse or any other evil entity, including masquerades and every evil human agent astral projecting, that wants to defile me, in the Name of Jesus.

Every evil altar that is projecting dream criminals, night caterers, night raiders, *spirit spouse* into my life, into my dreams, I destroy you now with the Thunder Hammer of God.

Lord, release me from the iniquity of every past sin that I've ever looked upon, thought of, or done every fornication, perversion, masturbation, incest, every form of immorality, in the Name of Jesus.

Every plantation of sexual immorality, come out with all your roots, in the Name of Jesus.

Bless the LORD, oh my soul and I command **all** that is within me to Bless Your Holy Name.

I cancel, nullify every polluted, demonic, masquerading, deceiving, dream criminal from the time that I first started dreaming – every evil dream from the time that I was born until now. I cancel and nullify every negative dream in the Name of Jesus.

I neutralize the effects of every evil polluted defiling dream against me, in the Name of Jesus.

I declare **DREAM IMMUNITY** by the Holy Ghost, in the Name of Jesus.

Lord, by Your Holy Spirit, help me flee foolish and youthful lusts, in Jesus' Name.

Lord, I shake off every evil *water spirit* out of my life, every one that is hindering my relationships, marriage, family, finances and overall successes of my life, in Jesus' Name.

Lord, I bind every evil marine and *water spirit*, so they have no effect on me anymore, no effect on anyone who is my intended, my fiancé, my beloved, my spouse to be, marriage partner, my kingdom spouse, in Jesus' Name.

Every fake relationship, fake marriage, all fake feelings brought on or allowed by *spirit spouse* get far away from me now by the Blood of Jesus, and the Sword of the Spirit.

Only real relationships, my real marriage, real emotions, and persons with Godly emotions toward me are allowed in my life from here on out, in the Name of Jesus.

Disappointments, divorce, unstable relationships--, I hit you, I bombard you now with Holy Ghost Fire, and I will not stop bombarding you until you're out of my life for good, in Jesus' Name.

I break and renounce all evil covenants with *spirit spouse* made between me and my father's or mother's house, in Jesus' Name.

I break and renounce the relationship between me and any *spirit spouse* sent by any witch or warlock, in the Name of Jesus.

My glory, my destiny, I retrieve you by Fire, in the Name of Jesus.

I cancel every polluted, defiled, corrupt, evil, demonic dream, in the Name of Jesus.

Spirit of lust, I bind your strong man, in the Name of Jesus.

Spirit of greed be bound, in Jesus' Name.

I recover by Fire all DNA from the scene of every indiscretion, in the Name of Jesus whether willing or forced, in rebellion or tricked, in the Name of Jesus. (X 7).

I repent and the Lord forgives me, Thank You, Lord.

Lord, expose the face of the *spirit spouse* by Fire and exile them for early torment and torture and then bury them alive, by Thunder, in the Name of Jesus.

My spirit, soul and body, be filled with the fire of the Holy Ghost, in Jesus' Name.

Any curse of fornication placed upon me by ancestral powers, I break your curse over my life, in the Name of Jesus.

I break every altar emanating curses, and I destroy every covenant that allowed any curse. I bind the demons assigned to enforce any, and every curse over my life, in the Name of Jesus.

I jump out of every spiritual dumpster, by FIRE in the Name of Jesus. Thank You, Lord.

Every *spirit spouse* eyeing my body, I blind you today, and I refuse to have relations with you, by Fire and by Force/ Lose my location and forget my coordinates. Receive the ARROW of God, dipped in the Blood of Jesus. DIE, in the Name of Jesus.

Every evil defiling mark placed on my body by any evil entity, especially marine water demons, *spirit spouses*, I blot you out by the Blood of Jesus.

Every evil bloodline or generational covenant with *spirit spouse* be broken today by the Blood of Jesus.

Father, I curse every *spirit* marriage to die by Fire, in Jesus' Name.

I declare divorce from every *spirit spouse*, in the Name of Jesus.

I shall not create or incubate any spiritual children with *spirit spouse* in the spirit, in the Name of Jesus. NONE! NOT ONE! NONE!

NO spirit child! NO *spirit child* to block or preclude my having natural children with my natural covenanted, God-ordained kingdom spouse, in Jesus' Name. Amen.

https://a.co/d/9f11n7u

Plans of *spirit spouse* over my life this year, I burn your evil calendar, and, with the Thunder Hammer of God I crush your evil clock, in the Name of Jesus.

Any curse against any organ of my body, break by Fire, in the Name of Jesus.

Bless the LORD, oh my soul, I command *all* that is within me to Bless His Holy Name.

My body, reject sexual covenant with any and every unclean *spirit* or evil human agent that has entered my life through intercourse or deception. Come out now, in the Name of Jesus.

Strongman from my foundation projecting strange people into my life in the dream, die, in the Name of Jesus.

Evil altar projecting strange people or demons into my life or dreams be shattered, crushed, annihilated by the FIRE of God, and be roasted to ashes, in Jesus' Name.

Lord God, arise and disgrace all foundational oppression against my destiny, in the Name of Jesus.

All evil spiritual food in my body, come out of your hiding places. Come out of every hiding place, in the Name of Jesus.

I drink the blood of Jesus. (X10)

Every satanic power, or evil human agent cooking up food for me, catch fire and explode, in Jesus' Name.

Every demon in the dream that wants to pollute my life, I bind you, in Jesus' Name.

Lord, set me free from every region of captivity so that I am **NOT** fed in the dream, so that I am not force fed in the dream, in the Name of Jesus.

Lord, make me mindful, even in the dream that I have choice, and I choose **not** to eat or drink anything at all in the dream. I am spirit, I do not need food in the dream. I do not live by bread but by every Word that proceeds from the mouth of God. Amen.

Bless the Lord, Oh my soul and I command **all** that is within me to bless His Holy Name.

I bind and totally destroy every link with dead people in my dreams, in Jesus' Name.

Every demonic dream attacking my finances be burned to ashes, in Jesus' Name.

Every satanic scheme that is attacking my business and career be shattered by thunder, in the Name of Jesus.

Every demonic dream fired into my life and destiny with intentions to derail my life, demote my life, or frustrate my life in any way, you are canceled and nullified, in the Name of Jesus.

Lord, every day of shame, disgrace, or any evil defiling dream targeting my life and future that brings me pain or bitterness of heart, I decree and declare that such a dream and such a day will never come to pass in my life, in the Name of Jesus.

Lord, do not let me be defiled with the *spirit of bitterness* of the heart. Give me power to forgive and to pull up and destroy every root of bitterness, in Jesus' Name.

Behold, Jesus stands at the door and knocks. I invite You in LORD JESUS, come in and dine with me, that I may live not just by bread alone, but by every Word that proceeds out of the mouth of God.

My spirit, be undefiled by sex, by sin and by food. My soul, be undefiled by sex, by sin and by food. My body, be undefiled by sex, by sin and by food. Lord, YOU prepare the table before me, in the presence of my enemies.

You, Lord, prepare the table before me in the presence of my enemies.

You, Lord, prepare the table before me even in the presence of my enemies so that I am not defiled, the food is not defiled.

Prophecy

And the Word of the Lord came saying to the saints of God, The things that happen to your body it is not old age, it is *old sin*. It is not old age, it is old sin, it is old *defilement*, it is <u>old food</u> that has been hidden in the body to program pain, and sickness and symptoms, disease and death in your body, in your joints, in your bones, and in your mind at a set time in your life.

Spiritual Surgery

Lord, destroy that evil calendar and that evil clock, in the Name of Jesus. You are the Great Physician, send a Holy Ghost stomach pump to remove all evil *spirit* food that I've consumed since birth until now, in the Name of Jesus.

Lord, send, seek, and find Holy Spirit missiles to find and fire upon and implode all hidden spirit food, every hidden defilement in my body, in the Name of Jesus.

Holy Ghost Fire. (X3).

Lord Jesus, send mighty angels to protect and comfort me, as You perform spiritual surgical excision of all hidden spirit food, and every weapon of defilement of the devil, in Jesus' Name.

Remove all hidden spirit food from my adrenals, arteries, back, bladder, blood, brain, calves, colon, digestive system, duodenum, ears, endocrine system, exocrine system, esophagus, eyes, fallopian tubes, fingers, feet, gall bladder hair, hands heart, intestines, jejunum, joints, kidneys, knees, legs, muscles, nails, nervous system, ovaries, pancreas, prostate, reproductive system, scalp, sinuses, skin, stomach teeth, throat, thyroid, tongue, veins, womb, and any other parts of my body that was not mentioned. Lord, by the Blood of the Lamb and by the Fire of the Holy Spirit and with surgical precision, remove every evil defilement that the devil has placed, lodged, hidden, and set in my body to use at a later time against me, in the Name of Jesus.

I repent of eating any and all defiling foods and accepting and/or ingesting any other devil weapon, in Jesus' Name.

Any way that I've defiled my body, Holy Ghost Fire, burn it up, in the Name of Jesus.

Lord, no weapon formed against me shall prosper. Lord, remove all old weapons of the devil that he has caused to be inside me, that I've foolishly, stupidly, ignorantly or by weakness ingested.

Lord, give me power and strength and Wisdom to know how to bless everything that goes into my body.

Bless the LORD, oh my soul and everything that is within me, everything that goes within me, Bless the Lord's Holy Name,

Lord, give me power, discernment, Wisdom to spit out everything that is not of you, not from you. *I proclaim all spirit food lukewarm,* evil, defiling and I reject it and I spew it out of my mouth, even in the dream, in the Name of Jesus. (X5)

Lord, whatever the enemy has captured of mine, whatever he holds captive, whatever he has that belongs to me, my life, peace, or destiny. Anything that the devil has captured by witchcraft, at any time, I recover all--, in the Name of Jesus.

Everything good that I have ever lost to the enemy through dreams since I was born up until now, I recover now by FIRE, by Thunder, by double Thunder, in Jesus' Name.

Fresh Fire of the Holy Ghost fall on me now for victory in every dream, in Jesus' Name.

Father, my God, I command all positive dreams to manifest in my life, in Jesus' Name.

Bless the Lord, oh my soul and I command **all** that is within me BLESS His Holy Name. Bless His Holy Name. (X3)

Thank You Lord, for sweet sleep, for sweet dreams, Holy Ghost inspired dreams, Bless the Lord, Oh My soul. Oh my soul, Bless Your Holy Name. **AMEN.**

Christian books by this author

Find these and many other titles by this author on amazon and Kindle and other platforms.

AK: The Adventures of the Agape Kid

AMONG SOME THIEVES

Churchzilla, *The Wanna-Be, Supposed-to-be Bride of Christ*

Demons Hate Questions

Don't Refuse Me, Lord (4 book series)

Evil Touch

The Fold (4 book series)

    The Fold (Book 1)

    Name Your Seed (Book 2)

    The Poor Attitudes of Money (Book 3)

    Do Not Orphan Your Seed

got HEALING? Verses for Life

got LOVE? Verses for Life

got money?

Let Me Have A Dollar's Worth

Man Safari, *The*

Marriage Ed. *Rules of Engagement & Marriage*

Made Perfect in Love

Power Money: Nine Times the Tithe

The Power of Wealth *(forthcoming)*

Seasons of Grief

Seasons of War *(forthcoming)*

The Spirit of Poverty *(forthcoming)*

Triangular Power *(series)*
- **Powers Above**
- **SUNBLOCK**
- **Do Not Swear by the Moon**
- **STARSTRUCK**

Warfare Prayer Against Poverty

When the Devourer is Rebuked

The Wilderness Romance *(3-book series)*
- *The Social Wilderness*
- *The Sexual Wilderness*
- *The Spiritual Wilderness*

Journals & Devotionals by this author:

The Cool of the Day – Journal

He Hears Us, Prayer Journal in 4 different colors

I Have A Star, Dream Journal kids, teen, adult

I Have A Star, Guided Prayer Journal, 2 styles:

J'ai une Etoile, Journal des Reves

Let Her Dream, Dream Journal

Men Shall Dream, Dream Journal, (blue or black)

My Favorite Prayers (multiple covers)

My Sowing Journal (in three different colors)

Tengo una Estrella, Diario de Sueños

<u>Illustrated children's books by this author:</u>
<u>Be the Lion (3-book series)</u>
<u>Big Dog (8-book series)</u>
<u>Do Not Say That to Me</u>
<u>Every Apple</u>
<u>Fluff the Clouds</u>
<u>I Love You All Over the World</u>
<u>Imma Dance</u>
<u>The Jump Rope</u>
<u>Kiss the Sun</u>
<u>The Masked Man</u>
<u>Not During a Pandemic</u>
<u>Push the Wind</u>
<u>Slide</u>
<u>Tangled Taffy</u>
<u>What If?</u>
<u>Wiggle, Wiggle; Giggle, Giggle</u>
<u>Worry About Yourself</u>
<u>You Did Not Say Goodbye to Me</u>

www.ingramcontent.com/pod-product-compliance
Lightning Source LLC
LaVergne TN
LVHW021409080426
835508LV00020B/2515